About the Author

Sara Evans is an award-winning freelance photo-journalist specialising in travel and wildife. She is a regular contributor to the *Sunday Telegraph* travel section and has also had work published in the *Independent on Sunday*, the *Independent on Sunday Review* magazine, *BBC Wildlife Magazine* and numerous other titles around the globe. Prior to working in journalism, Sara worked inhouse as head editor for a publishing company providing careers and education information for schools and colleges.

Acknowledgements

Sara would like to acknowledge the following:

- people1st whose research (Travel and Tourism Service Industry Report, March 2006) has been invaluable and is cited in the book

- Institute of Travel and Tourism

- AITO.

trotman

SARA EVANS

Travel Industry

UNCOVERED

Travel Industry Uncovered

This first edition published in 2006 by Trotman and Company Ltd
2 The Green, Richmond, Surrey TW9 1PL

© Trotman and Company Limited 2006

Editorial and Publishing Team

Author Sara Evans
Editorial Mina Patria, Editorial Director; Jo Jacomb, Editorial
Manager; Catherine Travers, Managing Editor; Ian Turner,
Editorial Assistant
Production Ken Ruskin, Head of Manufacturing and Logistics;
James Rudge, Production Artworker
Advertising Tom Lee, Commercial Director

Designed by XAB

British Library Cataloguing in Publication Data
A catalogue record for this book is available from the British Library

ISBN 1 84455 105 9

Typeset by Mac Style, Nafferton, East Yorkshire
Printed and bound by Creative Print and Design Group, Wales

CONTENTS

INTRODUCTION

IS THIS YOU?

Love the world you live in? Want to see more of it and want to help others see more of it too? Are you also a people person, organised, cheerful and enthusiastic as well as responsible? If you're nodding your head, then a career in travel could be for you!

The travel industry is an exciting and ever-changing industry to work in. It can offer plenty of rewards in terms of personal fulfilment as well as travel experiences but is one that demands commitment, long hours and flexibility.

CHANGING TIMES

Two decades ago, the travel industry was a very different industry to the one that it is now. Back then, most travel packages were targeted at two-week family holidays which were selected from a brochure and booked through a travel agent.

Today, people have a lot more choice about when and where they travel and what they do once they get to their destination. Of course, the original 'two weeks in the sun by the coast' packages still exist, but these days travellers can create an itinerary that can take in climbing mountains, meeting tribespeople, exploring diamond mines, planting forests and even translocating elephants!

The way that holidays are booked has changed too. Now all of the above can be booked without the need to ever speak with a travel agent. The rise of the internet means that travelling options can be explored, flights and accommodation booked and even itineraries created online, from home and at any time of the day or night.

QUICK BREAKS

Short-stay breaks are also increasingly popular. The growth of international budget flights has made it more possible for people to afford two or three shorter holidays, in different countries, rather than just one longer holiday in one destination.

Long haul flights to New York (USA) or even Cape Town (South Africa), for example, can be taken over a weekend. Tracking gorillas in central Africa can be done in three days as can silk buying in India. With many people finding it difficult to take a full two weeks off from their work, the few days they do get can be filled with some life-changing experiences.

GREEN BREAKS

And these life-changing experiences are not necessarily just for the tourists either. More and more tour operators provide holidays that give something back to the communities they visit. Monies from bookings are often put towards conservation and community initiatives or offer employment to local people. Some eco holiday companies even have environmental policies that help neutralise the 'carbon footprint' created by their clients as they fly off on their trips.

WANT TO BE PART OF THIS?

Unusual destinations, specialised activities and comfort and luxury while you do it are the driving force of today's travel industry. If you're excited to either help people book these sorts of holidays or be part of the teams that create niche and thoroughly organised itineraries, a career in travel can certainly take you places. Have a look at the quiz below to see if you are prepared for the kind of work you might have to do.

QUIZ – IS THE TRAVEL INDUSTRY FOR ME?
Are you prepared to:

● Learn at least one foreign language?

● Work long hours without regular breaks?

● Make frequent trips abroad?

● Have a smile on your face despite the fact that you're exhausted?

● Be flexible and willing to adjust your plans?

● Take responsibility?

If you've said 'yes' to all of the above, a career in travel could be just what you are looking for!

In the rest of this book, you can find out more about the travel industry, the jobs available and the employers who offer them. You can also find what qualifications and experiences you might need. And there are lots of suggestions on how you can make yourself the perfect candidate for a career in the travel industry. So what are you waiting for? Start turning the pages...

CHAPTER 1

Industry overview

Working in travel is a popular career choice making it a competitive arena in which to find a job. However, prospects for the industry are positive and a good number of vacancies come up year after year.

The information in this chapter provides you with an overview of the size of the industry as well as the sort of people who are employed in it.

IS THE TRAVEL INDUSTRY A STABLE ONE?

Yes, in recent years the number of employment opportunities has stayed at stable and healthy levels. The industry, along with the leisure and tourism sectors, employs around 1.9 million people. The industry is seen as a significant contributor of both jobs and wealth around the UK.

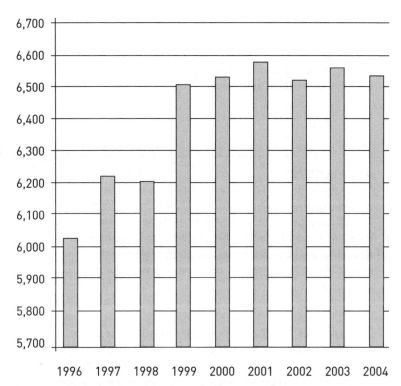

The graph above shows the total number of travel and tourist services enterprises from 1996–2004

Source: Annual business Inquiry, 2004

WHAT TYPES OF PEOPLE WORK IN THE INDUSTRY?

Of the approximately 110,300 people that work in travel and tourism, the following facts are known about them:

- The workforce is predominantly female – 72% of the workforce are women and 28% are men

- Most people work full-time – 27% work part-time

- Most are aged between 20 and 39

- 6% are from minority groups

- Around a tenth of workforce is self-employed

- 4% are in temporary employment – 52% of those in temporary employment say their work is seasonal while an additional 28% work on short-term contracts

- Full-time students make up 3% of the workforce.

ALL WELCOME
The travel industry is a very flexible area and one that often values experience and maturity above formal qualifications. This is good news for women returners and career changers. If you've a good travelling history and can demonstrate flexibility, responsibility and excellent organisational and people skills, there should be no reason why you don't get invited to as many job interviews as someone who is under 25 years old.

It is illegal for companies to discriminate against job candidates who may have disabilities. So job opportunities in the travel sector are available to people with disabilities. Find out more at www.drc-gb.org – the website of the Disability Rights Commission.

This chart shows that women make up a considerable majority of the people employed in the travel and tourism industry:

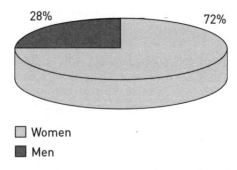

Employment by gender in the travel and tourism industry
Source: Labour Force Survey (LFS), 2004q2–2005q1

Here we can clearly see that the majority of jobs in this sector are full-time:

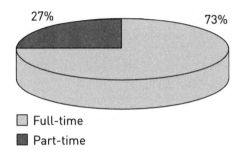

27%   73%

☐ Full-time
■ Part-time

Full- and part-time employment in travel and tourism
Source: LFS, 2004q2–2005q1

This graph indicates the range of ages of those employed in this particular industry:

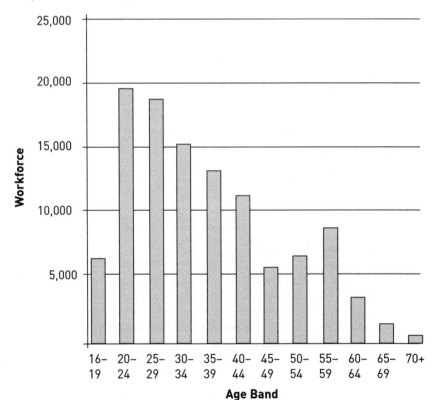

Ages of people working in travel and tourism
Source: LFS, 2004q2–2005q1

WHAT TYPES OF JOBS ARE THEY DOING?

- 40% are travel agents

- 6% are travel agency managers

- 9% are travel or tour guides

- The remainder are in related roles such as marketing, administration and customer care.

The table below shows the main occupations in the travel and tourism industry and the number of people working in them.

Occupation	Employment numbers	Percentage
Travel agents	42,513	39%
Travel and tour guides	9,828	9%
Travel agency managers	6,843	6%
General office assistants or clerks	4,738	4%
Marketing and sales managers	4,069	4%
Accounts wages clerk, bookkeeper	1,870	2%
Customer care occupations	1,721	2%
Marketing associate professionals	2,490	2%
Office managers	2,071	2%

Source: LFS, 2004q2–2005q1

NOTE ABOUT THE DATA
In this chapter you may have noticed that the data in the tables and charts refers to both the travel and tourism industries. This is because the Standard Industrial Classification (SIC) system used to collect data on industries combines the two and it is not possible to separate this information in half and use data that is specific only to the travel industry.

CONCLUSION

So now you have some idea of the types of job opportunities you might find within the travel industry as well as the sort of people you could be working with. Let's now find out in more detail about the jobs and the careers they might open up for you.

CHAPTER 2

The jobs

There are all manner of opportunities in the travel industry. Depending on what you want to do and the skills you have, you can be based in the UK in an office environment or in some faraway place looking for new experiences for others to enjoy. Although there are many other related roles, the key jobs are:

● Travel agency sales clerk (also known as sales consultant)

● Holiday representative

● Tour manager

● Tour operator.

This chapter explores each of these four roles in detail – letting you see just what the work and conditions are like, what the typical salaries are and the qualifications and qualities you need to get in. There are also a number of case studies to give you a really good insight into what jobs in travel are really all about. It also looks at some of the related occupations you may be interested in, and provides some hints and tips on carrying out a successful job search.

TRAVEL AGENCY SALES CLERK

WORKING AS A TRAVEL AGENCY SALES CLERK, WHAT WOULD I ACTUALLY DO?

Working in a retail outlet or call centre, you'd be promoting and selling package holidays and related travel services. In the main, you'd be dealing with customers: booking holidays, flights and accommodation to suit their needs and budgets.

If you choose to work in a travel agency that specialises in certain destinations or activities, you'd also be involved in helping your customers plan and create individual itineraries as well as booking local guides on their behalf.

Other duties you'd be expected to carry out include:

- Stocking shelves with new brochures and other promotional items

- Providing customers with various holiday options

- Suggesting destinations to match customers' interests

- Confirming the availability of holiday options with tour operators

- Filling in booking forms and collecting deposits

- Offering advice on activities, excursions and car hire

- Offering advice on passports, visa requirements, vaccinations and travel insurance

- Letting customers know when their tickets have arrived and collecting final payments

- Dealing with any complaints.

If you work in a call centre, you'd face similar tasks but deal with your customers over the phone rather than face-to-face. Agents specialising in business travel will also get involved with the planning and booking of trade fairs and conferences.

HOW MUCH CAN I EXPECT TO EARN?

Salaries vary from agency to agency, but, as this role is most often secured by school leavers, a junior travel agency sales clerk can expect to earn around £8,000 a year. Once experienced though, you could earn between £12,000 and £15,000. The most successful agents can earn up to £25,000 per year.

WHAT WILL MY WORKING CONDITIONS BE LIKE?

Typically, you'll work between 35 and 37.5 hours a week, usually covering five days between Monday and Saturday. There is normally a rota in place to provide cover for working on Saturdays. Some clerks also work on Sundays. During busy times or if you work in a major shopping centre, be prepared to work on a Sunday. In call centres, hours are similar but likely to be spread across a seven-day shift pattern.

Usually, the working environment is pleasant – working in a shop or office surroundings – sitting at a desk or counter. You will be expected to dress smartly. Some agencies may ask you to wear a uniform.

WILL I GET ANY TRAINING?

Yes, you will and most of it will be on the job. It will probably start with an induction course and then lead onto some specialist training and visits. It's also possible to work towards gaining the Association of British Travel Agents (ABTA) Travel Agents Certificate which can provide a good stepping stone towards gaining NVQ/SVQ levels 2, 3 and 4 in Travel Services.

ANY PERKS?

Many agencies, as part of a training package, may arrange for employees to visit resorts to improve their knowledge of the location. Travel within the UK may also be an option when attending short training courses.

WHAT QUALIFICATIONS DO I NEED?

Formal qualifications are not required, but GCSEs/S grades (A–C/1–3) in Mathematics, Geography and English are well received by employers. Strong personal qualities and enthusiasm are seen as very important. Experience of working with customers in a retail environment is also an advantage and will boost your chances of employment in this field.

Some employers may look for travel qualifications. See Chapter 4 for more information on these qualifications.

WHAT ABOUT SKILLS AND PERSONAL QUALITIES?

If you can demonstrate strong, positive evidence of these skills and qualities, potential employers will be delighted:

● Excellent communication skills

● Friendly, outgoing and polite

● Flexible and adaptable

● Able to cope under pressure

● Efficient

● Good phone manner

● Familiar with computers

● Good team worker

● Knowledge of global destinations.

AND INTERESTS?

Travel agency sales clerks who succeed in their jobs are normally interested in geography and travel as well as working with people and selling.

WHERE COULD THIS JOB LEAD ME?

It's possible to progress into a more senior role relatively quickly. If you work in a larger organisation, you could aim for branch manager status. Working for a smaller agency, you may find that you need to move companies to find promotion.

Some sales clerks go on to work for tour operating companies, often as holiday reps. Others find related employment working in travel marketing or other sales environments.

WHERE DO I FIND A JOB AS A TRAVEL AGENCY SALES CLERK?

Employed by travel agents, travel agency sales clerks can find jobs in small or large companies. Larger companies, especially the chains, tend to have more vacancies. A typical branch employs around three to six people while those working within internet or call centre functions may find themselves working with a larger number of colleagues.

Vacancies appear fairly frequently, but competition is stiff. Many of the larger agencies advertise their vacancies on their websites, but most post notices in local Connexions or Jobcentre Plus centres or in the local press.

WHERE CAN I GET MORE INFORMATION?

The Association of British Travel Agents (ABTA) is a good place to start:

68–71 Newman Street
London
W1T 3AH
Tel: 020 7637 2444
Website: www.abta.com

See also Chapter 6 for details on more helpful organisations and publications.

Now take a look at the case studies below to find out what those already working in this kind of job have to say about their work:

CASE STUDIES – TRAVEL AGENCY SALES CLERK

Ben Feetham – sales clerk for STA Travel

'Basically, I help customers plan and organise trips and holidays. I sell and arrange RTW (round the world) tickets, trips on the Eurostar to Paris and also organise accommodation, ground transport, package holidays and advise on passports and visas.

'I'm also involved in marketing too. In this role, I attend fresher and gap year fairs at universities, organise travel evenings and negotiate reciprocal marketing with local businesses.

'Since I booked my first trip with them, I've always wanted to work for STA Travel. I like the fact they organise a more independent style of travelling. Initially, I took a job in a high street travel agency to gain some experience whilst waiting for an opportunity for gaining employment with STA Travel.

'Of all my duties, I really enjoy booking interesting specialised trips for people who really appreciate all the effort that you put in for them. Managing to find trips that give the customer exactly what they are looking for is very rewarding.

'Keeping on top of the workload and ensuring that everything is done to a high standard is a key part of my role as is managing time constraints, reaching sales and revenue targets.

'As well as the daily challenges, there are also quite a few perks. For example, I recently won an incentive prize and went to Hong Kong for five days. I also receive a holiday allowance which is a sum of money given by the company to be spent on travel. There are also travel industry discounts and travel industry nights out with free drinks and prize giveaways.

'For people looking to work in a travel agency, I think it's important to realise the job can be stressful and to be aware that the job is very much a sales job. It's also a good idea to get some travel experiences under your belt (at least two continents) and if possible gain some sales work experience.

'In the future, I'd like to move overseas and set up a conservation tour operation (when I save up enough money!).'

Find out more about working for STA Travel by logging onto www.statravel.co.uk

Marianne Ward – group manager of a team of trainee travel agent sales clerks at Thomas Cook

'My role at Thomas Cook revolves around the training and development of staff including coaching, product training, sales techniques, performance reviews and appraisals and daily updates.

'I also provide staff with an update on sales performance and make sure that everyone knows what they are aiming for both individually and as a team. I also assist staff with questions and queries on how to find the perfect holiday for customers.

'As well as this, I liaise with managers and head office staff about what is working well within the team and how we can improve even more. I also co-ordinate cruise sales, ship visits and organise daily, weekly and monthly challenges to create a fun and competitive environment to increase sales of our packages.

'I got into my present role by seeing an advert in my local travel agency window. The vacancy looked interesting, so I applied and got the job. I worked through an apprenticeship for two years before becoming a sales consultant in a new sales centre. I then progressed to become a team leader when I went to work for Thomas Cook and I am now a group manager.

'I find my job really satisfying, and now I am in a management role I am excited at how my team has developed and am really proud of my staff. Prioritising duties can be challenging mostly because they change so often and I have to be on the ball.

'In the travel industry, world events can be challenging and often affect holiday destinations choices. Customers can become unsettled and world events can affect sales to certain destinations which makes it harder to achieve sales targets. We have to work with customers to suggest alternative destinations.

'The travel industry is always fast moving and changing and has always provided opportunities for further development and promotion. I am always doing something different and I never become bored. I get to see a lot of the world that I never would have done if I had not become a travel agent.

'I cannot think of any other sales role that would be more exciting, varied and sociable, or that provides the opportunity to travel to many destinations that you never normally go to. I started my career early but this does not have to be the case. If you are passionate about travel and learning, love talking to people and enjoy sales there can be no better experience than selling someone their dream holiday. If you get the opportunity, I would really recommend it.'

Find out more about working at Thomas Cook by logging onto www.thomascook.com

HOLIDAY REPRESENTATIVE (REP)

WORKING AS A HOLIDAY REP, WHAT WOULD I ACTUALLY DO?

Working as a holiday rep, you would be responsible for looking after holidaymakers at a particular resort, which is normally abroad. Holiday reps are also known as family reps, customer service reps, overseas reps or resort reps. Reps are the public face of holiday companies. Their main role is to make sure people who have booked a holiday with the company have a safe and happy holiday.

Your typical activities would include:

● Welcoming holidaymakers at the airport and taking them to their accommodation

- Holding induction meetings for new guests, providing them with information on things to see and do in their resort

- Selling additional company day trips, excursions and activities to holidaymakers

- Checking that holidaymakers are happy with their accommodation

- Updating noticeboards with information on day trips, special events etc

- Arranging car hire, taxis, sport equipment hire, foreign currency exchange

- Dealing with complaints and concerns of holidaymakers, and where necessary liaising with local medical staff, police and entertainment agencies

- Completing paperwork recording accidents, complaints etc.

If you choose to work as a children's representative, you would be involved in organising and supervising activities and games for young people so that their parents or carers can take a break. Some babysitting duties may also be required.

HOW MUCH CAN I EXPECT TO EARN?

You may find your starting salary working as a holiday rep fairly low – monthly pay packets normally hold around £450 to £500. Rates of pay do vary though, depending on the company you work for. It is likely that your accommodation and food will be provided (see below), so the money you earn seems relatively greater. If you work both winter and summer seasons, and have some experience, you could boost your income and earn up to around £15,000 a year.

WHAT WILL MY WORKING CONDITIONS BE LIKE?

Working away from home for months at a time, you'll find that as a holiday rep, your hours will be long and variable. Holidaymakers under your care will expect to be able to contact you 24/7 and you may have to work weekends as well as evenings. You can expect to get one day off a week, although you may be contacted in an emergency.

Holiday rep work is seasonal with the summer season being the busiest of the year. Normally starting in April, the summer season finishes around the end of October. The winter season runs from November to April.

The location of your resort will determine the type of climate and environment you could work in, but wherever you are based you can expect to work both indoors and out.

WILL I GET ANY TRAINING?

You certainly should. Most holiday reps have to complete a two- to four-week training course before they are sent to their resort. The training may be split – with half of it taking place in the UK and the remainder at the resort you'll be working in. Training will require you to become familiar with your resort so that you are able to provide holidaymakers with accurate and helpful information on things to do and see in the locality.

ANY PERKS?

Apart from having the experience of working abroad, you should find that your food and accommodation is all paid for by your employer.

WHAT QUALIFICATIONS DO I NEED?

Most employers look for applicants who are at least 21, although some may offer positions from age 18. There are no specific set entry requirements, but you would be expected to have a good all-round education. Some employers look for applicants who have some GCSEs/S grades (A–C/1–3), possibly in English, Mathematics and Geography.

Experience of working in a customer service role is seen as positive as is a working knowledge of one or more foreign language – especially Spanish, Italian, French, Greek or Portuguese.

Children's reps tend to be accepted from the ages of 18 or 19. Working in this role you would be expected to have a qualification in nursery nursing, such as a NNEB (National Nursery Examining Board) Diploma in Nursery Nursing or NVQ level 3 in Childcare. You will also be asked to have six months' experience working with children.

Many employers may look for specific travel-related qualifications or offer apprenticeships. See Chapter 6 for more information on these.

WHAT ABOUT PERSONAL SKILLS AND QUALITIES?

Working as a holiday rep, you'll need the following skills and qualities:

- Self-confidence

- Cheerful and outgoing nature

- A well turned out and groomed appearance

- Excellent communication skills

- Good organising skills

- Working knowledge of at least one foreign language

- Diplomacy and patience

- Be able to take responsibility and make decisions

- Be able to cope under pressure and deal with stress

- Be able to work alone as well as in a team

- Be healthy and resilient.

AND INTERESTS?

As a holiday representative, you'll be expected to have an interest in working with people and providing them with helpful services as well as showing enthusiasm for learning about other countries and their cultures.

WHERE COULD THIS JOB LEAD ME?

If you work in a larger company, there should be opportunities to gain promotion to more senior roles such as regional manager or team leader. Working for a smaller company, you may find promotion prospects a little harder to find.

After gaining experience, many travel reps go on to work in other areas of the travel industry becoming tour guides or working in resort or hotel management.

WHERE DO I FIND A JOB AS A HOLIDAY REP?

Vacancies for holiday reps tend to crop up fairly regularly. This is because many holiday reps only work for a few seasons before going on to try something different with the experience they have gained. Competition for jobs is strong with the numbers of people employed as holiday reps remaining relatively constant over the past few years.

Look on company websites for vacancies as well as travel trade journals such as *Travel Trade Gazette* and *Travel Weekly*. See Chapter 6 for more details.

WHERE CAN I FIND OUT MORE?

The organisation, Career in Travel, may be able to offer you more information about a career as a holiday rep:

Career in Travel
27 The Crossways
Chalvingtoncross
Chandlers Ford
Hampshire
SO53 2DP
Tel: 0870 744 1701
Website: www.careerintravel.co.uk

See also Chapter 6 for contact details of more helpful organisations.

CASE STUDIES – HOLIDAY REPRESENTATIVE

Leo Coney – loyalty manager, although many of his duties aboard a P&O cruise ship are similar to those of a holiday rep working aboard a cruise ship

'I originally joined a P&O cruise ship as a junior officer in the hotel department and really enjoyed the areas that allowed me to interact with the passengers. When the position of loyalty manager was advertised I jumped at the chance as the position really lends itself to passenger service and event management, which I really enjoy.

'My role is customer facing and includes activities such as managing our successful loyalty scheme, called The Portunus Club, organising all the onboard club events for members, socialising with our members at dinner, in port and at cocktail parties. Another important part of the role is to promote the Club to first-time cruisers. This is done by holding an event and then presenting to an invited audience.

'A vital part of the job is escorting the organised tours which passengers book onto. It's a great opportunity to spend time with passengers, to get to know each other better and, of course, it's a great way to see the city and surrounding areas that we are cruising by.

'I also really like the fact that I can have a direct positive effect on a passenger's cruise experience. With all the events that I organise for the passengers and the time that I spend with them, it's always good to hear they are having the holiday of a lifetime.

'In my position, one of the most challenging parts is meeting passengers' expectations. Often on longer cruises such as the World Voyages, passengers can have certain issues but it's my job to be diplomatic and suggest achievable solutions which are a benefit to the passenger.

'With any job you get the high times and low times and often it can be very hard working and living on board a super liner. It takes someone with dedication, pride and real passion in customer service to enjoy this lifestyle. If you are prepared to invest the time then the rewards are great.

'In the future, I would very much like to move further into marketing and develop my skills in event management that I have learned through my current role.'

Find out more about working for P&O cruises by visiting www.pocruises.com

Rachel Higham – ski resort rep for Inghams

'Typically, I provide advice and information for guests via my welcome meetings and hotel visits. I also sell and run day excursions and evening events (in summer) and après ski (in winter). As well as this, I also organise day excursions and ski passes, ski school and ski hire for guests.

'I'm also involved in liaising with suppliers (such as hoteliers, bus companies, hire shops and ski schools) and arranging transfers to and from the airport. I also keep the accounts for any excursions and ski packs sold to guests.

'I got into this line of work after studying in Austria. I liked it so much I really wanted to go back to Austria and work there. I also studied German as part of my degree and saw the job as an opportunity to improve my language skills too.

'My job is very busy, so not letting myself get too stressed when put in a pressurised situation is a key requirement of the work. For example, arranging ski passes, ski school and ski hire for over 50 people in under an hour and a half while on a bus certainly demands a cool head! The hours on arrivals days can be really long and by the end you can feel really knackered!

'However, the rewards of the job are fantastic. I find it really satisfying when guests tell me how much they have enjoyed their stay. Being able to live in such a beautiful country is wonderful. I also get to snowboard in my free time!

'For others looking to work as a ski resort rep, I would say that having a language really helps, as does some sort of background in customer service. A friendly personality and smile also help. I think you also have to have a genuine interest in people and when you are 'repping' it tends to show if you don't! Plus you do need to be very organised.'

Find out more about working at Inghams by logging onto www.inghams.co.uk

TOUR MANAGER/LEADER

AS A TOUR MANAGER, WHAT WOULD I ACTUALLY DO?

Tour managers travel with groups of tourists on their holidays – either overseas or within the UK. As a tour manager, you'd be responsible for ensuring that arrangements run smoothly, troubleshooting any problems that occur and also providing helpful information on places to visit, things to do as well as transport and accommodation options.

Administrative duties are a key part of the tour manager's job, so you should expect to get involved in all of the following:

● Welcoming tourists

● Checking tickets

● Checking accommodation details

● Making arrangements for meals and catering for travellers who may have special dietary requirements

● Booking and checking arrangements for visits to attractions

● Ensuring the itinerary is kept to

● Ensuring time is allocated for guests to transfer between various modes of transport

● Helping with problems such as lost luggage or accommodation issues

● Providing interesting commentary throughout journeys

● Organising additional excursions and activities as requested

● Keeping accurate records of tours, including any incidents that may have occurred

● Keeping accounts of any monies received or paid out.

HOW MUCH CAN I EXPECT TO EARN?

As a junior tour manager, expect to earn around £12,000 as your starting salary. With experience under your belt you could earn up to £25,000 a year. You'll find that salaries vary depending on the types of tour and company that you work for. Most tour managers tend to work on a freelance or on a short contract basis.

WHAT WILL MY WORKING CONDITIONS BE LIKE?

Your working conditions will depend on the type of tour you manage. So, for example, if you are working on a coach tour then a large amount of your time will be spent aboard coaches. This could be just for a few days or for over a month. Working on other types of tours, you could be based on trains, cruise ships, planes or a combination of all of these. The location and climate of countries you are touring will all determine the type of outdoors environment you operate in.

Regarding hours, tour managers often find themselves – for the duration of the tour – on call 24/7 and starting early and finishing late. As soon as you first meet your party, you are then responsible for them until the end of the tour, so work hours are intense. While on tour, you are expected to work weekends with no days off. You should also expect to be away from home for days or weeks at a time.

Most tour managers find that summer is the busiest time, so it's likely that you'll find most of your work during April to October. This is known as the summer season. The winter season is from November to April.

WILL I GET ANY TRAINING?

Yes, you should do. Most new tour managers receive an induction course covering the destinations covered by their tour operator. You would be expected to learn about all the areas and attractions taken in during tours. You also need to be prepared to update this knowledge regularly.

While working, you may be able to study towards NVQ/SVQ levels 2 and 3 in Travel Services (Commentaries and Interpretation for Tourism), and levels 3 and 4 (Tour Operations). See Chapter 4 for more information on travel-related qualifications.

If you decide to work on European tours, you will be expected to have a Tour Manager's Certificate (TMC). This is issued by the International Association of Tour Managers (IATM): contact details are given on page 29. The TMC is available for free to active members of the IATM. The IATM also offer an accreditation scheme – the CTM (Certificate of Tour Management) examination – open only to association members working as tour managers.

ANY PERKS?

As well as visiting foreign countries, you should find that the tour operator you work for will pay for your flights to meet and leave tours. You should also receive free board and lodging and be able to claim for related expenses.

WHAT QUALIFICATIONS DO I NEED?

To work as a tour manager, you'll find that there are no formal entry requirements. Many tour operators see strong people skills as highly important although they may prefer candidates with these skills as well as some GCSEs/S grades (A–C/1–3).

Some employers may look for staff with a degree, but this is mainly for specialist tour operators who are looking for employees with a specific knowledge base such as History of Art, for example.

If you want to work abroad as a tour manager, then having a foreign language qualification under your belt will be extremely useful.

Some employers may also appreciate specific travel-related qualifications or offer apprenticeships. See Chapter 6 for more information on these.

WHAT ABOUT SKILLS AND PERSONAL QUALITIES?

For tour managers, these are just as important as qualifications. Successful tour managers need:

- Excellent communication skills

- A warm and approachable manner

- Self-confidence and a smart appearance

- Good report writing and IT skills

- To be responsible and make decisions

- To be flexible and adaptable to change

- To be able to cope with stress and work well under pressure

- To be able to work well without supervision

- To be able to develop a thorough knowledge of tour destinations

- To be able to work long and irregular hours.

AND INTERESTS?

Successful tour managers are usually interested in travel, learning about new cultures and working with people.

> ### FASCINATING FACTS
>
> **Entry for people over the age of 24 is certainly possible as most travel-related jobs and courses have no upper age limit attached to them. In fact, if you have spent time travelling or working in a related environment, you may find that employers will value both your maturity and your experiences. The Travel Training Company (TTC) offer, at their discretion, some funded places for applicants over the age of 24. See Chapter 6 for TTC contact details.**

WHERE COULD THIS JOB LEAD ME?

After managing a series of successful tours, you may be invited to continue working freelance for a particular tour operator. On this basis, you may be able to select the tours you work on. With experience, you may be able to develop your own tours and start up your own tour operation business.

It's also possible to move into working as a tourist guide or into other areas of travel, hotel or resort management. You could move into more office-based work for a tour operator in the UK if you want a rest from travelling.

WHERE DO I FIND A JOB AS A TOUR MANAGER?

Tour managers are employed by tour operators which can be large international companies or small, specialist enterprises. As a tour manager, you are likely to work freelance and be employed on a tour by tour basis by these companies.

Generally, there are plenty of vacancies which appear regularly due to the short-term nature of the work. However, competition is strong as this is a popular area to work in. In recent years, the number of jobs in tour management has remained stable.

Tour managers jobs are often advertised on the websites of tour operators and in specialist publications such as *Travel Weekly* and the *Travel Trade Gazette*. See Chapter 6 for details of these websites and publications.

WHERE CAN I GET MORE INFO?

The International Association of Tour Managers Limited (IATM) will be able to provide you with more information:

IATM
397 Walworth Road
London
SE17 2AW
Tel: 020 7703 9154
Website: www.iatm.co.uk

See Chapter 6 for other helpful organisations and publications.

Now take a look at these case studies to see what those already working in this type of job have to say about their work.

CASE STUDIES – TOUR MANAGER/LEADER

Richard Beal – tour leader in Europe for Explore

'I work abroad leading tours for Explore around Europe. These tours are sympathetic to local eco needs, culture and customs. Problem solving, arranging tours and local guides as well as providing passengers with local information and giving short informative talks are all a key part of my role.

'I've always loved travel and travelled as much as I could before starting work. I have a keen interest in wildlife, culture and religion but also enjoy being with people. I applied for this role at Explore when I saw the job advertised in a travel magazine. At the time I had just come back from South America and didn't want to return to shop work – I had previously worked in an outdoor clothing shop where it was so depressing selling stuff to people going to amazing countries while I was stuck indoors in the shop!

'Probably one of the main things I enjoy about the job is the sense of achievement I get, especially after finishing a series of tours. I also enjoy receiving comments from passengers

---

about having a great holiday. Meeting and mixing with local people is great and witnessing the interaction of passengers within societies is a real joy. It's great when you can make a difference by changing someone's perception of a culture.

'Starting a tour is always difficult for me. I get nervous and always worry as to how passengers will see me and get along. However, I always want do my best and my passengers leave with the best experience of the country possible.

'For me, a real perk of the job is obviously the travel, but also getting the chance to work in other countries alongside local people is amazing. Being in the country for a longer period of time is also good.

'For others interested in this type of work I would say keep travelling to as many countries as possible. Enjoy the travelling and learn from your experiences so that others can learn from these later. Organisational skills are also very important.

'For the time being, I am happy working in this role. Maybe one day though, I'll help plan a new tour or even work in the office, but I will have to wait as when you have the best job in the world, what can you do next?'

Find out more about working at Explore by logging onto www.explore.co.uk

Anna Raven – tour manager with Travelsphere

'My main role is to ensure my customers have the best holiday experience possible during their time with me. I spend a great deal of time reading up on the culture and history of all the places I visit to ensure I impart as much information as possible to customers. I provide detailed commentary on places of interest whilst on tour.

'I also discuss the planned itinerary in great detail with my group and ensure my customers know where they need to be and at what time. I research local doctors, hospitals and emergency services too and arrange excursions with local guides and establish timings with coach drivers.

'I am also responsible for all accounting whilst on tour, which entails collecting monies for excursions, paying entrance fees to attractions and museums, preparing an accounting spreadsheet for all banking activities. On occasion, I am a shoulder to cry on – at times it is important to reassure customers, offer encouragement and provide assistance for those with limited mobility.

'From a young age, I have always wanted to travel and held a particular desire to climb Mount Kilimanjaro, a dream which was fulfilled in March 1999. The expedition was led by a tour manager who did not inform, advise or support us throughout the entire trip. By the end of the trek, I'd made up my mind that this was what I wanted to do although much, much better. I called Travelsphere, who are local to me and they invited me in for an interview.

'Working here has many advantages such as getting to travel but working with people is also great. You tend to form relationships with customers – many of mine I now consider friends. The knowledge that I don't work in a typical 9–5 job is also great. Each day is different, I could be in New Zealand one week or guiding a tour through the 'Lost City' of Machu Picchu in Peru in the next.

'For people looking to get into this line of work, I'd say it is important to have a passion for travel and a love of people. It is also helpful to be fit – as there's a great deal of walking, running around, late nights and early mornings. Being organised is also vital and if possible learn a few languages, particularly Spanish.

'Also research the area of travel you want to go into as each offers different opportunities and take time to research the companies you would initially like to send your CV to.'

Sally Hewerston – general manager at Steppes Travel

'On a day-to-day basis, I manage the sales team and the sales support team. I also deal with clients – either by phone or email – and put together tailor-made itineraries for them. I also deal with suppliers including airlines, hotels and ground agents. As well as this I book flights, hotels and make other ground arrangements for my clients. I also do my best to keep up-to-date with new developments in countries I handle.

'I would say that the most challenging aspect of my job is ensuring that all details dovetail with each other regardless of how many countries are involved. Doing this ensures that nothing is missed that may cause a problem for travelling clients. Making sure all the details are checked and double-checked (and checked again) is imperative!

'I think that having an excellent attention for detail is a must-have skill for this type of job. Confidence in dealing with people and loving other cultures is also important.

'For me, the most enjoyable part of my job is putting together a trip for happy clients and adding special details that make a client's holiday something different and memorable. I also love the fact that I can visit new countries I've not been to before.'

Find out more about working for Steppes Travel at www.steppestravel.co.uk

TOUR OPERATOR

AS A TOUR OPERATOR, WHAT WOULD I ACTUALLY DO?

Tour operators are the people who put package tours together either for holidays or business trips. These are then either sold to the public or to other companies to sell on.

Working as a tour operator, you'd be expected to get involved in the following:

- Planning, researching, visiting and checking venues, hotels, restaurants and sightseeing tours

- Reviewing sales, quality and profitability of existing holiday packages, and taking on board customer feedback

- Developing and improving existing holiday packages, and when required, recommending the dropping of less viable and less popular packages

- Negotiating provisional costs and booking with airlines, hoteliers, coach operators and venues

- Continual liaison with airlines, hoteliers, resort reps etc to ensure operations are running smoothly and to budget

- Organising the issuing of tickets and invoices either directly to customers or via travel agents

- Preparing marketing materials and websites and organising any related new tour launches

- Coming up with ideas for new and interesting packages that give your operator a competitive edge.

HOW MUCH CAN I EXPECT TO EARN?

Salaries vary widely from tour operator to tour operator. Typically though, you can expect a starting salary of between £13,000 and £20,000 per annum. With experience and a proven track record, by the age of 40 you could expect to earn from £25,000 to £40,000.

WHAT WILL MY WORKING CONDITIONS BE LIKE?

Much of your time will be spent sitting behind a desk in an office. While sitting there, you'll be using IT skills to research new packages, evaluate existing ones and prepare reports and presentations. Hours are likely to be 9 to 5, working five days a week.

When not behind your desk, you may spend time travelling to new destinations and checking what they have to offer. Climate and environment will depend upon your destination although you will probably be working both indoors and outside.

WILL I GET ANY TRAINING?
The type of training you may receive depends largely on the company you work for. Most operators do offer training which tends to be run in-house and short in duration. Typical courses would cover sales, customer care, finance and IT.

There is also an industry-recognised qualification known as the Certificate in Travel (Tour Operators). This qualification tests the knowledge and skills required for working in tour operations. Its components include:

● Travel destinations

● Travel industry

● Tour operator's services

● Legislation

● Ticketing

● Package holiday

● Emergencies and problems.

ANY PERKS?
As a tour operator, you are likely to get paid expenses to visit new destinations around the globe.

WHAT QUALIFICATIONS DO I NEED?
To be a tour operator, there are no set standards as such. However, many employers favour people with a degree or HND, especially in one of the following subjects:

● Travel and tourism

● Hotel/catering management

- Business-related subjects

- Language-related subjects

- Marketing

- IT.

However, not having a degree does not rule you out by any means. Candidates with a good educational background, relevant experience and good organisational and foreign language skills are always sought after.

Apprenticeships are available and other travel-related qualifications are also a plus. See Chapter 4 for more details on these sorts of qualifications.

WHAT ABOUT PERSONAL SKILLS AND QUALITIES?
Good tour operators have the following skills and qualities:

- Strong organisational skills

- Ability to work under pressure to deadlines

- Proven customer service skills

- Excellent communication skills

- Commercial awareness

- Marketing skills

- IT skills.

AND INTERESTS?
Most successful tour operators are interested in travel, other countries, working with people and developing new travel experiences.

WHERE COULD THIS JOB LEAD ME?

In tour operations work, the prospects available vary widely from company to company. The larger organisations will offer more promotion prospects than the smaller ones. Within the larger organisations, there is also more scope for moving into different types of management roles. Many experienced tour operators go on to set up their own tour operation businesses.

WHERE DO I FIND A JOB AS A TOUR OPERATOR?

Jobs in this line of work are competitive and you will require related on-the-job experience for most positions. Many holiday reps go on to become successful tour operators. It's true that there are a few very large tour operating companies, but most tend to be small and specialist, hence the need for experience.

You can find vacancies on tour operators' websites. These are the website addresses for the UK's four largest tour operators:

- TUI: www.thomsontravelgroup.com

- My Travel: www.mytravelcareers.co.uk

- Thomas Cook: www.thomascookjobs.com

- First Choice: www.firstchoice4jobs.co.uk

Vacancies also appear in the *Travel Trade Gazette* and *Travel Weekly*. See Chapter 6 for contact details of more employers.

WHERE CAN I FIND OUT MORE?

The Association of Independent Tour Operators (AITO) may be able to provide you with more information:

AITO
133A St Margaret's Road
Twickenham
Middlesex
TW1 1RG
Tel: 020 8744 9280
Website: www.aito.co.uk

See Chapter 6 for details of other helpful organisations and publications.

Now read about this case study to see what one tour operator has to say about their job.

CASE STUDY – TOUR OPERATOR

Liz Dempsey – assistant director of independent tour operator Wind, Sand and Stars

'Wind, Sand and Stars specialises in providing tours in remote areas of Egypt, usually taking in time with tribal people of the region. My role as assistant director requires that I fulfil a number of duties. These include taking responsibility for sales, our marketing and website and managing our staff in the office and out in the field.

'I'm also responsible for managing our legal and operations requirements. Since we have a variety of clients, setting up journeys for many diverse groups is always a challenge, but an enjoyable one! We aim to make other people's dreams a reality, as well as working with local Bedouin tribes to offer visitors a unique insight into such a rich cultural history and beautiful landscape.

'I really enjoy seeing the joy on clients' faces after spending time in a totally different environment and culture. Also, I enjoy the close relationships and trust we have built over the years with the local communities and the satisfaction of knowing that the company gives something positive back towards a sustainable lifestyle for the Bedouin.

'If you are looking for a career as a tour operator, then I would suggest that you travel as much as you can. If you want to specialise in ecotravel always try to travel with companies who have good eco-friendly policies and who give back to the communities in which they work.'

RELATED OCCUPATIONS

So far, this chapter has looked at the main roles available in the travel industry. But there are many more related jobs that are just as interesting. AITO (the Association of Independent Tour Operators), for example, gives the following overview on the type of roles available working for a tour operator:

- **Reservations consultants:** a good way in to start. Generally lower paid but with good sales incentives.

- **Holiday representatives** (or tour manager for coach tours): the best way to find out how tour operating really works and good experience for using later in management. Can be stressful!

- **Operations:** the engine room of the tour operating office. Need good methodical organisational skills eg bookings for airlines, hotels, transfers etc and logistics of getting people from reservations consultants to holiday representatives. Can also be stressful!

- **Product management and contracting suppliers:** usually natural course of progression from holiday representatives or working in operations.

- **Marketing:** depending on the size of the company, there may be assistant roles available plus management posts. Is increasingly web driven although print (brochures etc) is still used.

- **Field sales:** if the company actively sells through travel agents, it will probably have sales people looking after them. You will need a driving licence as this involves visits of agents around the UK.

- **Accounts:** qualified accountants are required by all types of companies working in the travel industry

- **IT:** databases, office systems, websites

- **Customer and legal services:** looking after customers is key to the growth of successful tour operators while those with a legal background (especially specialising in areas of international law) will find openings with some of the larger operators.

AITO also comments that:

'Depending on the size of the company some of the roles
described below can be combined. In the main, smaller operators
want quick thinking generalists who thrive on multitasking and
can cope under pressure!'

You can find out more by logging onto www.aito.co.uk or by
attending travel trade exhibitions; the Tourism Society should have
details of forthcoming events on their website,
www.tourismsociety.org. To give you a taste of what's out there, the
following paragraphs take a more in-depth look at just one of the
related occupations that may be of interest to you: travel
media/marketing and travel writing/photography.

TRAVEL MEDIA/MARKETING

Working in the travel media sounds rather glamorous, but it is
highly competitive and extremely demanding work. Typical travel
media employers are the big tour operators, tourist offices and
boards, airlines and public relations companies. Typical jobs include
working in-house for a company or handling accounts for a PR
company. Your duties would revolve around securing as much
favourable publicity as possible for your client or company's tours
and travel services.

In this line of work, you'll be expected to be full of ideas as well as
to have a working knowledge of dealing with publicity materials,
understanding print, layout and production procedures and budgets.
Many people move into this line of work after working in journalism.

TRAVEL WRITING/PHOTOGRAPHY

These are often regarded as the ultimate travel jobs. Be warned
though – it is a very, very competitive arena to work in and the
financial rewards are not great. You can enter the profession by
training with the National Council for the Training of Journalists
(see Chapter 6 for contact details) or by sending in
submissions/digital photographic files on spec. Getting related work
experience is key as is perseverance.

COULD YOU MAKE IT IN TRAVEL MEDIA/WRITING?

Can you say yes to all of the questions below? If you can, a career in the travel media could be for you...

● Can you take negative criticism?

● Do you have a thick skin?

● Are you creative and bold?

● Do you persevere and have stamina?

● Are you willing to keep checking facts, presentations etc

● Do you have an elephant's memory for facts and figures?

Now take a look at these case studies to find out what those already working in this area think about their jobs.

CASE STUDIES – TRAVEL MEDIA/WRITING

Ian Ripper – director of Guerba and responsible for the marketing of the company's tours

'I'm responsible for all marketing and PR of Guerba. This means that I choose the media we want to work on, get creative adverts done and work on the web with portals seeking search engine optimisation and maximising other online activities. I also deal with email and printed mail direct marketing.

'As well as this, I meet the press and get stories related to Guerba published by organising press trips. Regarding travel exhibitions, I also choose which travel shows to work with and design stands.

'My connection with Guerba started in 1998 when I worked for them as an overland driver. I then worked in Guerba in Kenya for seven years before doing a long-distance MBA and returning to UK as partner and director for marketing.

'Developing Guerba's website has been a great challenge and a real learning experience. I also enjoy being able to do lots of good things such as getting 7000 trees planted in Africa through our carbon compensation scheme, getting funding to build a children's home in Tanzania through our charity climbs on Kilimanjaro – these things really make a difference to people.

'To people looking to work in the industry, I would suggest that although adventure travel is fun and rewarding, working in travel is not just about spending huge amounts of time abroad – it's also an opportunity to make a difference to people's lives through good travel policies that are actually implemented.'

Emma Coburn – product and marketing manager for Kumuka Worldwide

'Working for Kumuka Worldwide, my typical activities are varied and interesting. I am involved in our advertising, promotional campaigns and events as well as our brochure production. I am also a contributor to *Venture* magazine and also co-ordinate the implementation and promotion of new and amended tour products. As well as this I am also involved in our website development and content, corporate relationships, affiliate partnerships, sponsorships and travel shows.

'I started travelling when I was 17 and fell in love with it, both as a lifestyle and as an industry. Travel influences people's lives to an enormous extent, and provides the scope for amazing experiences. It also assists them in gaining a global appreciation of the world they live in. I wanted to be a part of an industry that made this possible, while contributing to it in a responsible and sustainable way to ensure that tourism not only benefits travellers, but also the communities, cultures and environments that host them. Marketing was personally the most interesting medium through which I wanted to achieve this.

'To help achieve this, I completed degrees in tourism management and marketing, and then found a graduate position at Qantas Airways in their sales and marketing division. After three years in this job, I left Qantas as I wanted to work in adventure travel.

'Believing my passion for exploring the more remote areas of the world could translate into my work, I approached Kumuka Worldwide. I applied without a vacancy being advertised, but was lucky enough to be employed after a successful interview. I became the product manager at Kumuka, before also taking over the marketing division for the company.

'If you'd like to get into this line of work, then it helps to get experience of the industry as a consumer, ie get out there and travel so that you understand the industry from that point of view. Know yourself and the people you meet along the way as 'customers' so that you are familiar with what needs are to be met as a 'provider'.

'My own experience as a traveller comes in handy every single day in my job when making major decisions. If you don't understand your 'typical' customer, chances are you will miss the mark.

'Also don't wait around for advertised positions. Decide who you are most interested in working for, and start making contact. Also be prepared to begin in different or lower positions and work your way up.'

TOP TIPS ON GETTING A JOB IN THE TRAVEL INDUSTRY

BE CONVINCING
If you are keen to specialise in a certain area like conservation or in sporting holidays, you must be able to demonstrate that you have a keen interest in that employer's specialist areas. Join relevant clubs and societies. Also take part in some related volunteering activities. Then add these specialist experiences to your CV and be prepared to talk about them with both passion and authority.

DON'T GIVE UP
Finding a job in travel is competitive. There are lots of lovely roles wanted by lots of lovely people! The trick really is to keep trying. Many small travel agencies and operators may not advertise widely, so contact them first, send in your CV on spec and be prepared to work for companies that you may not have considered at first.

USE THE WEB
Use the internet to research your options and look for vacancies. The website www.tourismtraining.biz holds the details of over 500 travel-related companies. You can also use the web to design yourself an inexpensive business card. It's important to develop contacts and networks in this type of industry.

LOOK IN THE RIGHT PLACES
It's estimated that around a quarter of travel-related jobs are posted in local job centres. Take a look at Chapter 5 for more details about building up your CV so that your job application has the best chance of success.

GETTING INTO TOUR OPERATING

AITO (Association of Independent Tour Operators) offers some tips for getting into tour operating work:

- Travel around the world – experience of other countries relevant to a company is very valuable, especially for the smaller specialist tour operators

- A degree helps if you aim to progress into management, preferably a degree in tourism management, languages or business/marketing

- Think about the type of tour operator you would like to work for – it helps to be passionate about the product and the interviewer will pick this up. Research on the web for the type of tour operator you want to work for and apply to them first

- Don't write standard application letters/emails – make it personal to the operator's needs and product.

Find out more about AITO by logging onto www.aito.co.uk

CHAPTER 3

The employers

In Chapter 2 we saw the main jobs in the travel industry. The table below shows you the typical employers who recruit people in these roles:

Role	Type of employer
Travel agency sales clerk/consultant	Travel agent – can be a high street chain or small independent outlet
Holiday representative	Mainly tour operators – usually on a freelance or contract basis
Tour manager	Mainly tour operators – usually on a freelance or contract basis
Tour operator	Tour operator or self-employed

This chapter will look in more detail at travel agents and tour operators, using real companies as examples to give you an idea of the diversity of the industry.

TRAVEL AGENCIES

Travel agencies are companies that recruit travel agents to sell the holidays put together by tour operators. Holidays are usually sold as a package and include accommodation and transport options.

Agencies can be owned by individuals as a small business or be part of a high street chain and seen in most cities or towns around the country. Chain agencies are often owned by a large tour operator. Thomson Holidays are a good example of a chain.

Travel agencies recruit travel agency sales clerks/consultants but they also recruit people in the following roles:

● Accounting and finance

● Business and marketing

● Administration

● Management

● Secretarial.

The following profiles should give you a taste of a few travel agencies and the kind of work available with them. See the Further Information chapter for listings and contact details of more travel agents.

TRAVEL AGENCY – INDEPENDENT
Name of company: Trailfinders
Based: 16 travel centres in the UK, one in Dublin and five in Australia
Established: 1970
Number of employees: Over 1000
What does the company actually do? Arranges tailor-made independent travel to destinations worldwide
Typical offering: Air New Zealand round-the-world trip from and to London, with stops in Hong Kong, Auckland and Los Angeles
What types of jobs could I get with the company? Travel consultant, sales supervisor, ticketing supervisor, administration (in London and Oxford)

Any other interesting facts I should know about?

● Books more UK passengers to Australia than any other travel company in the UK

● Has travel centres in Ireland and in Australia

● Allows one period of sabbatical leave for each member of sales staff

● All staff benefit from free meals at work

● Receives 50,000 telephone calls per week and has a website receiving 80,000 hits per week

● Has been voted Best Travel Agent seven times by *Guardian* and *Observer* readers and Best Independent Travel Specialist by readers of the *Telegraph* for five years in a row.

How do I contact them?
Trailfinders
42–52 Earls Court Road
London
W8 6FT
Tel: 020 7795 8000
Website: www.trailfinders.com

TRAVEL AGENCY – CHAIN
Name of company: Going Places
Based: Over 500 stores in the UK and Ireland
Established: 1973 (as Airtours)
Number of employees: Over 10,000 in the UK and Ireland
What does the company actually do? Sells package holidays, villa stays, cruises, city breaks and flights
Typical offering: Two-week self-catering holiday to the Oro Blanco studios and apartments in Playa de las Americas, Tenerife
What types of jobs could I get with the company? Cabin crew, customer service representative, entertainer, nursery nurse, overseas administrator, travel advisor, holiday money advisor, store manager

Any other interesting facts I should know about?

- Part of the MyTravel Group Plc, with 81 hotels, 31 aircraft and over 700 stores worldwide

- Has 3.4 million customers in UK and Ireland

- Also part of the MyTravel Group are Airtours Holidays, Panorama Holidays, Direct Holidays, Cresta Holidays, Escapades, Aspro Holidays, Manos Holidays and Tradewind.

How do I contact them?
Going Places Leisure Travel Limited
Holiday House
Sandbrook Park
Rochdale
OL11 1SA
Tel: 01706 742000
Website: www.goingplaces.co.uk

TOUR OPERATOR/TRAVEL AGENCY – CHAIN
Name of company: Thomson Holidays
Based: Over 730 travel shops in the UK
Established: 1965
Number of employees: 3000
What does the company actually do? Offers package holidays, cruises, city breaks, winter sports and villa stays
Typical offering: seven nights self-catering at the Cancun Clipper Club, Cancun, Mexico
What types of jobs could I get with the company? Resort representative, chalet host, children's representative, nursery nurse, resort administrator, resort manager, entertainment host, store manager, sales consultant, IT, resort catering and hotel staff, resort walking guide, water sports instructor.
Any other interesting facts I should know about?

- Sells around five million holidays and flights each year

- The majority of the company's employees work overseas

- Has one-third of the UK market share

- Sister company is Thomsonfly.com, the UK's third largest airline

- Other brands include Jetsave & Jersey Travel, Simply Travel, Headwater Holidays, Magic Travel Group, Crystal Holidays, Thomson Ski & Snowboarding, Thomson Lakes & Mountains

- Is part of TUI AG, the world's largest travel organisation.

How do I contact them?
Thomson Holidays
Wigmore House
Wigmore Place
Wigmore Lane
Luton
LU2 9TN
Tel: 0845 055 0255/0845 055 0258
Website: www.thomson.co.uk

FASCINATING FACTS

ABTA (The Association of British Travel Agents) is the main trade association for tour operators and travel agents in the UK. In total 1052 tour operators and 6310 travel agency offices are ABTA members and are responsible for selling around 85% of holidays sold in the UK. Try to find work with companies that are members of ABTA.
(Source: ABTA website, 23/01/05)

TOUR OPERATORS

Putting package tours together for holidays, tour operators either sell these direct to the public or to travel agencies and coach companies amongst others. These packages usually consist of accommodation, transport, transfers as well as the services of reps.

In the UK, the tour operating industry is divided into three sections. The table below demonstrates this sector split:

Sector	Customers and related info
Outward bound holidays	Operators in this sector devise holiday packages for British people wishing to travel abroad. Many of them are members of the Association of Independent Tour Operators (AITO)
Incoming visitors to the UK from abroad	These tour operators provide packages and services for international visitors to the UK. They tend to be members of the British Incoming Tour Operators' Association (BITOA)
Holidays in the UK for British people	Typical companies include canal boat operators, weekend break providers, coach and bus companies

Like travel agencies, tour operators can either be large, national organisations or small independent companies, possibly specialising in a particular area. Typical specialisms are listed below:

- Cycling

- Walking

- Wildlife and nature

- Climbing

- Cultural tours

- Historical tours

- Family holidays

- Singles or couples holidays.

The profiles below illustrate just how diverse a tour operator's specialisations can be. See the Further Information chapter for listings and contact details of more tour operators.

TOUR OPERATOR – INDEPENDENT
Name of company: Audley Travel
Based: Stratton Audley, Oxfordshire
Established: 1996 (as Asian Journeys)
Number of employees: 120
What does the company actually do? Sells tailor-made trips to destinations around the world. Destinations include southeast Asia, Indian subcontinent, Africa, North Africa and Arabia, South America, Antarctica, New Zealand, the South Pacific and Australia
Typical offering: Uzbekistan Uncovered – ten-day trip to Uzbekistan's Silk Road. Optional add-on trips include camel-trekking in the Kyzylkum Desert and visiting the stranded ships at the retreating Aral Sea
What types of jobs could I get with the company? Country specialist, reservations ticketing administrator, marketing, accounts
Any other interesting facts I should know about?

- Ranked in the top 10 of tour operators by readers of *Wanderlust* magazine

- Company has been highly ranked for the last two years running in the *Sunday Times* '100 Best Small Companies To Work For' survey

- All members of staff have the opportunity to participate in educational trips overseas

- All staff have either lived in or travelled through the regions that they operate in

- The company supports these charities: Friends of Conservation, Climate Care, Schools for Children of Cambodia, Encompass Trust and Task Brazil.

How do I contact them?
Audley Travel
6 Willows Gate
Stratton Audley
Oxfordshire
OX27 9AU
Tel: 01869 276222
Website: www.audleytravel.com

ONLINE TRAVEL/TOUR OPERATOR – INDEPENDENT

Name of company: The Russia Experience
Based: Perivale
Established: 1994
Number of employees: four
What does the company actually do? Arranges trips on the Trans-Siberian Railway
Typical offering: 12-day snow train trip on the Trans-Siberian Express from Moscow to Beijing, including sightseeing in Moscow, a stop to see Harbin and a visit to the Harbin Ice and Lanterns Festival
What type of job could I get with the company? Sales consultant
Any other interesting facts I should know about?

- Has a sister company, Beetroot Backpackers (www.beetroot.org), offering budget itineraries for travel in Russia

- Supports the work of The Railway Children (www.railwaychildren.co.uk), a charity assisting runaway and abandoned children who inhabit the world's railway stations.

How do I contact them?
The Russia Experience
Research House
Fraser Road
Perivale
Middlesex
UB6 7AQ
Tel: 020 8566 8846
Website: www.trans-siberia.com

SPECIALIST TOUR OPERATOR – INDEPENDENT

Name of company: Wildlife Worldwide
Based: Alresford
Established: 1992
Number of employees: Eight
What does the company actually do? Offers tailor-made wildlife holidays around the world
Typical offering: 11-day trip to Tanzania to witness the spectacular mass migration of over one million wildebeest on the Serengeti, staying in a mobile tented camp, visiting Kilimanjaro and finishing at Ngorongoro Crater Lodge
What types of jobs could I get with the company? Specialist sales consultants, operations assistants
Any other interesting facts I should know about?

- The Wildlife Worldwide Group consists of Wildlife Worldwide, Walks Worldwide, Dive Worldwide and Equine Adventures

- The company organises an annual Festival of Wildlife, which features renowned wildlife experts such as Jonathan and Angela Scott, David Shepherd OBE, Stephen Mills and Mark Carwardine

- Supports a number of charities and organisations including the David Shepherd Wildlife Foundation and the Kapani School Project in Mfuwe, Zambia

- All clients booking a holiday with Wildlife Worldwide are offered automatic membership to the David Shepherd Wildlife Foundation.

How do I contact them?
Wildlife Worldwide
Long Barn South
Sutton Manor Farm
Bishop's Sutton
Alresford
Hampshire
SO24 0AA
Tel: 0845 130 6982
Website: www.wildlifeworldwide.com

WHAT ARE TRAVEL EMPLOYERS LOOKING FOR?

According to the Institute of Travel & Tourism, top employers in the industry are looking for people who can demonstrate all of the following skills and qualities:

● Good communication skills – both written and verbal

● Good basic geographical knowledge

● Good at dealing with people

● Able to adapt to any situation quickly

● Must be able to handle pressure

● Able to work well under own initiative or as part of a team

● Have a love of travelling and experiencing new cultures – or the desire to do so!

● Positive personality

● Previous customer service and selling experience an advantage.

See Chapter 5 for more detailed information on building up your CV to make sure you have just the skills and experiences that your employer will be looking for.

COULD YOU WORK FOR A SPECIALIST TRAVEL AGENCY OR TOUR OPERATOR?
If working in an environment that specialises in travel to a particular country or region appeals to you, see if you can say yes to all or most of the questions below:

● Can you speak the language/s spoken there?

● Are you a good communicator?

- Can you demonstrate a real passion for the area that will translate into sales?

- Are you prepared to stand up in front of a crowd and deliver a presentation on the region?

- Are you prepared to work long hours?

CHAPTER 4

Routes in

QUALIFICATIONS AND TRAINING

Further education providers find that travel and tourism courses are some of the most popular around. There are certainly a good number of courses to choose from too. In fact, currently, there are around 98 qualifications related to the travel, tourism and leisure sector in England. Most of them are level 3 qualifications. There are also six Scottish Vocational Qualifications (SVQs) in tourist information services and travel services (tour operations).

Qualification level	Number of qualifications
Entry	2
Level 1	14
Levels 1 and 2	6
Level 2	28
Level 3	44
Level 4	4

Source: QCA, OpenQUALS database, November 2004

People working in the travel and tourism industry tend to be well qualified. Of the total workforce, around 80% are qualified to level 4, level 3 and level 2 (see box below to explain qualification levels). Around 10% are qualified to level 1 while 5% have no qualifications. The graph below shows this more clearly.

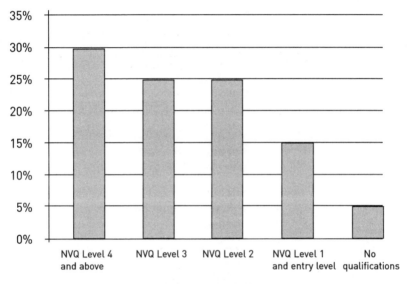

Qualification profile of the UK travel and tourist services workforce
Source: LFS, 2004q2–2005q1

EXPLAINING QUALIFICATION LEVELS

Level	Qualification
Entry level	Basic literacy and numeracy qualifications
1	GCSEs (grades D–G) 1 NVQ at level 1 1 level 1 certificate or equivalent
2	5 GCSEs (grades A–C) 1 NVQ at level 2 1 Intermediate GNVQ or equivalent
3	2 GCE A levels (or AS equivalent) 1 NVQ at level 3 1 Advanced GNVQ or equivalent
4	1 NVQ at level 4 Certificate of higher education or equivalent
5	Diplomas of higher education and further education Foundation degrees Higher national diplomas
6	Bachelor degrees Graduate certificates and diplomas
7	Postgraduate certificate/diploma Master's degree
8	Doctorate

But although there are so many qualifications available, there is no one set formal qualification required to work in the travel industry. You need to be sure that the qualification you opt to study is one that matches the needs of your future employers. Follow these tips to help ensure you opt for the right courses:

- Speak with the personnel staff working at potential employers about the type of qualifications they favour

- Ask college staff if their courses match up with your career plans

- If possible, try and speak with ex-students of the courses you are interested in to find out where they ended up working

- Find out if the area you want to work in favours courses with more work experience than paperwork – or vice versa.

FASCINATING FACTS

As a member of the travel and tourism workforce, you're likely to receive more training than people working in other sectors! According to the Labour Force Survey, 26% people in travel and tourism services were involved in some sort of job related training in the last 13 weeks – the average elsewhere in the UK workforce was 23%.

TYPES OF COURSES

The courses outlined below can be helpful for finding work in the travel industry.

ACADEMIC/VOCATIONAL QUALIFICATIONS

- **GCSE:** Leisure and Tourism

- **Apprenticeship in Travel Services:** there are no set entry requirements but you need to be aged between 16 and 24, not in full-time education and be living in England

- **BTEC First Diploma in Travel and Tourism:** entry requirements are usually four GCSEs (D–G) or equivalent

- **BTEC National Diploma in Travel and Tourism:** entry requirements are a BTEC First Diploma in Travel and Tourism in a related subject or four GCSEs (A–C) or equivalent

- **NVQs/SVQs levels 2, 3 and 4 in Travel Services:** no set entry requirements

- **SQA National Modules in Tourism or Travel and Tourism:** entry requirements are four GCSEs/S grades (A–C/1–3) plus one A-level/two H grades or equivalent

- **Higher National Certificate/Diploma in Tourism or Travel and Tourism:** entry requirements are four GCSEs/S grades (A–C/1–3) plus one A level/two H grades or equivalent

- **BTEC HNC/HND in Travel and Tourism Management:** entry requirements usually ask for three GCSEs/S grades (A–C/1–3), including English and Mathematics, plus one A level/two H grades or equivalent

- **AVCE in Travel and Tourism:** (double award)

- **Foundation/Higher education degrees in travel and tourism or similar:** entry requirement is usually a minimum of two A levels/three H grades or equivalent along with five GCSEs/S grades (A–C/1–3) or equivalent

- **Postgraduate courses:** entry requirement is a higher education degree.

PROFESSIONAL QUALIFICATIONS
Travel agency or tour operator work:

- ABTA Travel Agents Certificate (ABTAC) in Travel (travel agency)

- ABTA Certificate in Travel (tour operators)

- Also consider apprenticeships, NVQs/SVQs in administration and call centre qualifications. IATA Air Fares and Ticketing Courses available at foundation, primary and advanced levels.

Holiday representative work:

- Consider short courses in first aid, basic hygiene and relevant sports qualifications (eg British Association of Snowsports Instructors (BASI) if you want to work in a ski resort)

- Consider NVQ/SVQ in customer care.

Children's Holiday representative work:

- NNEB or NVQ/SVQ in childcare or CCE (Childcare and Education Certificate).

DEGREE COURSES

Although a degree is not necessary to enter a career in the travel industry, it may be a great aid to securing a job. It may enable you to enter at a higher level, especially if the degree programme involves a work placement, giving you experience working in the sector. Degrees can also improve your promotion prospects. See below for a list of universities and colleges offering relevant degree programmes.

LEARNING A LANGUAGE

Language skills are highly valued by travel employers. If you are not learning a language at school or college, contact the Centre for Information on Language Teaching (CILT, see Chapter 6 for contact details) for information on finding a language course. Popular languages to study include Spanish, Arabic, Mandarin and French. Also consider Russian, Polish and Korean.

MORE INFORMATION?

To find out more about the qualifications outlined above, check out the following websites:

- For GCSEs, NVQs/SNVQs, A levels/Highers: City & Guilds www.city-and-guilds.co.uk; Edexcel www.edexcel.org.uk; OCR www.ocr.org.uk

- For apprenticeships: www.apprenticeships.org.uk

- For professional certificates: Travel Training Company
  www.ttctraining.co.uk

- For foundation/higher degrees: UCAS www.ucas.com.

WHERE TO STUDY?

Many of the above courses will be on offer at your local school or college of further education. If you are interested in taking a degree, here is a list of higher education institutions offering travel-related degrees.

Institution	Website
University of Wales, Aberystwyth	www.aber.ac.uk
Basingstoke College of Technology	www.bcot.ac.uk
Bath Spa University (formerly Bath Spa University College)	www.bathspa.ac.uk
University of Bedfordshire	www.beds.ac.uk
Bell College	www.bell.ac.uk
Birmingham College of Food, Tourism & Creative Studies	www.bcftcs.ac.uk
Blackpool and the Fylde College An Associate College of Lancaster University	www.blackpool.ac.uk
Bournemouth University	www.bournemouth.ac.uk
Bradford College	www.bradfordcollege.ac.uk
University of Bradford	www.bradford.ac.uk
University of Brighton	www.brighton.ac.uk
City of Bristol College	www.cityofbristol.ac.uk
University of the West of England, Bristol	www.uwe.ac.uk
Brockenhurst College	www.brock.ac.uk
Buckinghamshire Chilterns University College	www.bcuc.ac.uk
University of Central Lancashire	www.uclan.ac.uk
Chichester College	www.chichester.ac.uk
City College Manchester	www.ccm.ac.uk
City of Sunderland College	www.citysun.ac.uk

Coventry University	www.coventry.ac.uk
Craven College	www.craven-college.ac.uk
Dearne Valley College	www.dearne-coll.ac.uk
University of Derby	www.derby.ac.uk
Doncaster College	www.don.ac.uk
Ealing, Hammersmith and West London College	www.wlc.ac.uk
Exeter College	www.exe-coll.ac.uk
Glasgow Caledonian University	www.gcal.ac.uk
University of Greenwich	www.gre.ac.uk
Guildford College of Further and Higher Education	www.guildford.ac.uk
Highbury College Portsmouth	www.highbury.ac.uk
Hull College	www.hull-college.ac.uk
University of Kent	www.kent.ac.uk
Park Lane College, Leeds	www.parklanecoll.ac.uk
Leicester College	www.lec.ac.uk
London Metropolitan University	www.londonmet.ac.uk
London South Bank University	www.lsbu.ac.uk
Loughborough College	www.loucoll.ac.uk
Middlesex University	www.mdx.ac.uk
Neath Port Talbot College	www.nptc.ac.uk
Newcastle College	www.ncl-coll.ac.uk
New College Durham	www.newdur.ac.uk
New College Nottingham	www.ncn.ac.uk
University of Northampton	www.northampton.ac.uk
Northbrook College Sussex	www.northbrook.ac.uk
Northumbria University	www.northumbria.ac.uk
North Warwickshire and Hinckley College	www.nwhc.ac.uk
Pembrokeshire College	www.pembrokeshire.ac.uk
Salisbury College	www.salisbury.ac.uk
Solihull College	www.solihull.ac.uk
Somerset College of Arts and Technology	www.somerset.ac.uk
Southampton Solent University	www.solent.ac.uk
South Cheshire College	www.s-cheshire.ac.uk
Staffordshire University	www.staffs.ac.uk
University of Sunderland	www.sunderland.ac.uk
Swansea Institute of Higher Education	www.sihe.ac.uk

University of Teesside	www.tees.ac.uk
Thames Valley University	www.tvu.ac.uk
Tyne Metropolitan College	www.tynemet.ac.uk
University of Ulster	www.ulster.ac.uk
University of the Arts London	www.arts.ac.uk
Warwickshire College	www.warkscol.ac.uk
Westminster Kingsway College	www.westking.ac.uk

NB: this listing is not comprehensive and only shows the institutions currently providing courses, not the course titles as these are subject to change. Please check www.ucas.com for details and to find entry requirements. Please also note, that tourism can be combined with all sorts of degree subjects.

MATURE ENTRY

All the courses covered in this chapter are open to adults of all ages. Some employers may offer you work even if you don't have the qualifications they require. This may be because they value your experience over formal qualifications. Be prepared though to take top-up or short courses. If you are considering a degree, contact individual institutions to find out if they offer mature students alternative entry requirements.

CHAPTER 5

Next steps

So, you've read all about the industry and the jobs now, and you might well be convinced that working in travel is definitely something you wish to pursue. But how do you convince future employers that you are the one to employ out of the many other applicants who have applied for the same job?

Well, apart from having any necessary qualifications (see Chapter 4), having the right personal qualities and skills is just as important. In this chapter, you'll find an overview of the particular skills and qualities that are favoured for each of the four job types covered in Chapter 3 plus some helpful tips and suggestions on how to gain them.

Remember, the more skills and qualities that you are able to acquire and add to your CV, the more likely you are to impress travel industry employers.

OVERVIEW OF SKILLS/QUALITIES PREFERRED IN THE TRAVEL INDUSTRY

Favoured skills and personal qualities	How to get them
People facing	● Get work experience or a part-time job in a shop or restaurant. Or, if you're really lucky, within a travel agency or tour operator. Look for their contact details in your local newspaper or *Yellow Pages* ● Let your Connexions or career advisor know that you want to work in travel so they can help organise relevant work experience placements
First aid	Take a basic first aid course. If you belong to an organisation such as the Scouts or Guides, you may be able to take a course with them. Otherwise contact your local Connexions centre. They will be able to advise you on local, short courses
Interest in the world	● Travel as much as you can – abroad and in the UK ● Take courses/lessons in anything related to the cultures of other countries. Spanish dancing, martial arts, Indian cooking or North American history are all examples of the type of thing you could study ● Subscribe to and read *National Geographic* or other similar publications ● Visit museums and galleries that have international exhibits – remember what you saw there and what insight it gave you into other cultures
Helpful, cheerful nature	● Help out at charity events ● Join an organisation such as the Scouts or the Guides

- Volunteer at an old people's or children's home
- Join a local conservation group
- Get testimonials from the group/s you join pointing out your positive qualities

Stamina, perseverance, takes responsibility
- When you join or get involved with any of the above, ensure you stay committed for at least a year. Try to gain positions of responsibility while there
- At school or college, try to become a prefect or have a responsible role in a club or society

Foreign language
Either choose a GCSE language option/s at school or attend night classes at your local college

BECOMING A TRAVEL AGENT SALES CLERK: CHECKLIST

Tick off the following suggestions to help you demonstrate your suitability for becoming a travel agent to future employers. As you achieve these goals, add them to your CV.

Things to do	Achieved
Get an atlas and familiarise yourself with the world's continents and major capital cities	☐
Buy and read travel magazines/books	☐
Try to visit other places – they can be in the UK or abroad	☐
Remember where you have been and note down the most memorable aspects of the trip	☐
Log on to travel websites to see the type of holiday packages on offer. Look to see how different travel agents may offer specialised packages and activities to suit the specific needs of certain customers	☐
Try to get some work experience either in a travel agents or other retail outlet	☐

BECOMING A HOLIDAY REP: CHECKLIST

Tick off the following suggestions to help you demonstrate your suitability for becoming a holiday rep to future employers. As you achieve these goals, add them to your CV.

Things to do	Achieved
Study at least one foreign language	☐
Buy and read as many travel magazines and books as you can	☐
Try to join a club or society where you can take on a responsible role that involves organising people and arranging trips	☐
Look for a Saturday job where you can gain confidence working with people and develop good people skills. If you want to work as a children's rep, look for babysitting opportunities	☐
Try to get some work experience in a UK resort. You may also be able to find summer jobs here	☐

BECOMING A TOUR MANAGER: CHECKLIST

Tick off the following suggestions to help you demonstrate your suitability for becoming a tour manager to future employers. As you achieve these goals, add them to your CV.

Things to do	Achieved
If possible study a language at school or try a home study course	☐
Buy and read travel magazines/books	☐
Go on a tour – either in the UK or abroad – and take notes on exactly what the tour offers and how the tour manager works	☐

Things to do	Achieved
Look for a Saturday job where you can gain confidence working with people and develop good people skills	☐
Try to get some work experience with a local tour manager or in a local tourist attraction	☐

BECOMING A TOUR OPERATOR: CHECKLIST

Tick off the following suggestions to help you demonstrate your suitability for becoming a tour operator to future employers. As you achieve these goals, add them to your CV.

Things to do	Achieved
Study a foreign language. If possible, try to study for a travel-related qualification or degree (See Chapter 6 for more info on helpful qualifications)	☐
Buy and read travel magazines/books	☐
Travel as much as you can – in the UK and abroad. Be able to talk enthusiastically and accurately about your travels. Consider how your experiences could form the basis of a new tour. Write out an itinerary – potential employers may be impressed by an original and well thought through one	☐
Log on to travel websites to see the type of holiday packages on offer. Look to see how different travel agents may offer specialised packages and activities to suit the specific needs of certain customers	☐
Find a short term job in a travel-related environment – consider working as a holiday rep or tour guide	☐

CASE STUDIES

Read the case studies in Chapter 3 again – they each offer advice and tips on getting in to the travel industry from people already working successfully in that area.

CREATE A CV FOR THE TRAVEL INDUSTRY

Having a relevant CV is essential for impressing future employers. In most cases, your CV is the first contact that an employer has with you. From this, employers have to decide whether to invite you to an interview and then, possibly, to offer you a job.

Travel industry recruiters are busy people and won't have the time to spend working out what skills you may or may not have or whether you are really interested in a job in the travel industry. Your CV must sing out with the fact that you are the perfect candidate and make it easy for them to see this. One look at your CV and they should be putting you down as a definite person to interview.

This might sound easier said than done, but with the right approach and the right content to put on your CV, the procedure shouldn't be too difficult or time consuming.

Assuming that you've taken up some of the suggestions outlined earlier in this chapter, you just need to get these experiences clear and transparent on your CV. Do this by indicating clearly what experiences you have gained and how these have equipped you with the necessary qualities.

The CV below is one that has been created by an imaginary candidate called John Livingstone. Take a look at it to see how his experiences have been translated into the sort of evidence that most employers will be delighted to see.

CURRICULUM VITAE OF JOHN LIVINGSTONE

Address: 12 Livingstone Way,
Little Acorn Town,
Cambridgeshire
CB99 9ZZ

Date of birth: 12/12/1986
Tel: 098273 37822221
Email: jlivingstone@
acornsforever.com

Qualifications:

- GCSE, grade C, in Mathematics – taken in 2002
- GCSE, grade C, in English Literature – taken in 2002
- GCSE, grade B, in Geography – taken in 2002
- GCSE, grade B, in Italian – taken in 2002
- First Aid certificate, commended – taken in 2003
- A level, grade B, in Italian – taken in 2004
- A level, grade C, in Geography – taken in 2004.

Volunteering and work experience:

- Three-week work experience placement with Sun City Breaks – 2001
- Volunteer at Seigfried's Retirement Home – 2001 until 2004
- Saturday job at Sun City Breaks – 2002 until 2004
- Volunteer at Vatican City Restoration Unit, Rome, Italy – summer of 2005
- Volunteer at Cape Town City Hospital, South Africa – spring of 2006.

Travelling experience:

- Followed own itinerary, travelling across Europe, spending four months in Italy – September 2004 to mid-2005
- Followed own itinerary, travelling across Africa, spending three months in South Africa – mid-2005 to July 2006.

Skills and qualities:

- Flexible and adaptable
- Can think on feet

- Good organiser
- Motivated and helpful
- Quick learner
- Committed and have stamina
- Friendly and cheerful.

Interests:

- Travelling
- Learning new languages
- Working with people from other cultures and countries
- Finding out more about the world
- International cuisine
- Swimming and diving.

Referees:

- Mrs C Clark, Manager, Sun City Breaks, 12 Under Wood Way, Little Acorns Town CB99 9ZX Tel: 098273 37822229
- Mr J Priestly, Volunteer Co-ordinator, Cape Town City Hospital, Westbrook, Cape Town, South Africa Tel: 0027 9873 93722259.

YOUR LETTER OF APPLICATION

The letter that accompanies your CV is just as important as your actual CV. You need to keep the letter brief and to the point but also use it to link up with your CV, making it totally clear why you are the best candidate for the job.

The application letter here is written by the imaginary John Livingstone and is a good example of a competent application letter. Read and note how it focuses on the writer's experiences and skills that are directly relevant to the job applied for. It also clearly states the name of the job being applied for and where the vacancy was posted.

If you are applying by email, the same principles apply. Email may seem a more informal way of communicating but when you are applying for a job, you still need to adopt a formal and respectful approach.

LETTER OF APPLICATION

12 Livingstone Way
Little Acorn Town
Cambridgeshire
CB99 9ZZ

Ms Susan Ward
African Explorers
22 Borchette Drove
Little Acorn Town
Cambridgeshire
CB1 8XX

25 August 2006

RE: Tour Manager vacancy

Dear Ms Ward,

I am applying for the Tour Manager vacancy as advertised in the *Little Acorn Courier* on Wednesday the 23rd of August.

I believe that I am a strong candidate for the role for a number of reasons. I have just returned, for example, from a year-long trip through Africa during which I visited a number of countries and became familiar with various cultures and landscapes. I also volunteered for three months in a hospital in Cape Town, South Africa which gave me a unique insight into this fascinating country.

Prior to my African trip – which I organised myself – I travelled through Europe under my own steam. This first trip equipped me with the necessary skills that made my journey through Africa run smoothly and to plan.

Prior to my travels, I worked part-time for Sun City Breaks where I gained a good working knowledge of the travel industry and the skills required to play a valuable role in it.

You will see from my enclosed CV that I have been interested in travel from an early age and that I have now developed the necessary skills and experiences to make a positive and enthusiastic contribution, as an employee, to African Explorers and, as a tour manager, to your clients.

I look forward to hearing from you.

Yours faithfully,

John Livingstone

Well, now you have read this book you should be ready to get out there and start looking for your perfect travel job. Follow the advice we have given you and be confident! Good luck!

CHAPTER 6

Further information

Use the contact details in this chapter to find out more about working and securing the career you want in the travel industry.

TRAVEL ORGANISATIONS

ABTA (Association of British Travel Agents)
68–71 Newman Street
London
W1T 3AH
Tel: 020 7637 2444
Website: www.abta.com

AITO (Association of Independent Tour Operators)
133A St Margaret's Road
Twickenham
Middlesex
TW1 1RG
Tel: 020 8744 9280
Website: www.aito.co.uk

CIMTIG (Chartered Institute of Marketing Travel Industry Group)
c/o CIM
Moor Hall
Cookham
Maidenhead
Berkshire
S16 9QH
Tel: 01628 427500
Website: www.cimtig.org

GTMC (Guild of Travel Management Companies)
Queens House
180–182 Tottenham Court Road
London
W1T 7PD
Tel: 020 7637 1091
Website: www.gtmc.org

Irish Travel Agents Association
Heaton House
32 South William Street
Dublin 2
Eire
Tel: 00 353 1 679 4179
Website: www.itaa.ie

NAITA (National Association of Independent Travel Agencies)
Kenilworth House
79–80 Margaret Street
London W1N 7HB
Tel: 020 7323 3408
Website: www.advantage4travel.com

People1st
2nd Floor
Armstrong House
38 Market Square
Uxbridge
UB8 1LH
Tel: 0870 060 2550
Website: www.people1st.co.uk

EMPLOYERS LISTING

Although the listing here is not comprehensive, it gives you a good idea of the type of employers operating in the travel industry. Many employers post their vacancies on their websites as well as information about their company objectives and services.

AA Appointments (AGENCY)
Tel: 020 7480 7506
Website: www.aaappointments.com/uk

Abercrombie & Kent (COMPANY)
Tel: 01242 547700
Website: www.abercrombiekent.co.uk/about/careers/

Adventure Jobs (WEBSITE)
Tel: 0870 202 0121
Website: www.adventurejobs.co.uk

Anywork Anywhere (WEBSITE)
Website: www.anyworkanywhere.com

Arctic Experience (COMPANY)
Tel: 01737 214214
Website: www.arctic-experience.co.uk/DTW/vacancies.asp

Argyle Travel Recruitment (AGENCY)
Tel: 020 7580 1876
Website: www.argylerecruitment.com

Audley Travel (COMPANY)
Tel: 01869 276216
Website: www.audleytravel.com/index.php/about/workforaudley/current-vacancies/

Aviation Jobsearch (WEBSITE)
Website: www.aviationjobsearch.com

BA Recruitment (COMPANY)
Tel: 0870 608 0747
Website: www.britishairwaysjobs.com

Barefoot Traveller (COMPANY)
Tel: 020 8741 4319
Website: www.barefoot-traveller.com/job.asp

BMI (AIRLINE)
Tel: 01332 854000
Website: www.flybmi.com/bmi/en-gb/aboutbmi/recruitment/recruitment.aspx

Bourne Leisure Limited (COMPANY)
Tel: 01442 230300
Website: www.bournejobs.co.uk

British Mediterranean Airways (AIRLINE)
Tel: 020 8630 4000
Website: www.british-mediterranean.com/recruitment.php

C&M Travel Recruitment (AGENCY)
Tel: 020 7796 1800
Website: www.candm.co.uk/travel/default.asp

Carlson Wagonlit Travel (COMPANY)
Tel: 01707 667741
Website: www.carlsonwagonlit.com/en/countries/uk/careers/

Casino Cruise Jobs (WEBSITE)
Tel: 078 9996 8790
Website: www.casinocruisejobs.com/index.cfm

Cheapflights.co.uk (WEBSITE)
Website: www.cheapflights.co.uk/careersatcheapflights/

Cosmos Holidays (COMPANY)
Tel: 0871 423 8422
Website: www.cosmos-holidays.co.uk/jobs.php

Cox & Kings (COMPANY)
Tel: 020 7873 5000
Website: www.coxandkings.co.uk/General/Jobs.aspx

Dragoman Overland (COMPANY)
tel: 01728 862255
Website: www.dragoman.com/workforus/index.php

Easyjet (AIRLINE)
Website: http://easyjet.com/EN/Jobs

Ebookers.com (WEBSITE)
Website: http://careers.ebookers.com

Eurostar (COMPANY)
Tel: 01777 777878
Website: www.eurostar.com/UK/uk/leisure/about_eurostar/employment.jsp

Exodus (COMPANY)
Tel: 020 8675 5550
Website: www.exodus.co.uk/vacancies.html

Expedia.com (COMPANY)
Website: www.expediajobs.com/?loc=eu

First Choice (COMPANY)
Tel: 0870 750 1204
Website: www.firstchoice4jobs.co.uk/fe/tpl_firstchoice01.asp

First Choice Holidays (COMPANY)
Tel: 0870 750 1204
Website: www.firstchoice.co.uk/info/aboutus/careers.cfm

Flight Centre Limited (COMPANY)
Website: http://careers.flightcentrelimited.co.uk

Flybe (AIRLINE)
Tel: 01392 366669
Website: www.flybe.com/vacancies/default.htm

Forces Holidays (COMPANY)
Tel: 0870 240 1132
Website: www.forcesholidays.com/employment.php

Gecko Travel (COMPANY)
Tel: 023 9225 8859
Website: www.geckotravel.com/jobs.php

Global Choices (COMPANY)
Tel: 020 7433 2501
Website: www.globalchoices.co.uk

Global Holidays (TRAVEL AGENTS)
Tel: 0870 199 9038
Website: www.globalholidays.co.uk/travel-agent-jobs.htm

Global Village Travel (COMPANY)
Tel: 0870 442 4848
Website: www.globalvillage-travel.com/staff.asp#workGV

Global Vision International (COMPANY)
Tel: 0870 608 8898
Website: www.gvi.co.uk/pages/recruitment.asp

Great Cruise Jobs (WEBSITE)
Tel: 01483 791291
Website: www.greatcruisejobs.co.uk

Hays Travel (COMPANY)
Tel: 0191 510 5155
http://careers.haystravel.co.uk

Headwater Holidays (COMPANY)
Tel: 01606 720006
Website: www.headwater.com/all/work/index.htm

Holiday Resort Jobs (WEBSITE)
Website: www.holidayresortjobs.co.uk

Holidaybreak plc (COMPANY)
Tel: 01606 787522
Website: www.holidaybreakjobs.com

Inntravel (COMPANY)
Tel: 01653 617949
Website: www.inntravel.co.uk/careers.htm

Intrepid Travel (COMPANY)
Tel: 020 7354 6169
Website: www.intrepidtravel.com/employment.php

i-to-i (COMPANY)
Tel: 0800 011 1156
Website: www.i-to-i.com

Jobs in Travel & Tourism (WEBSITE)
Website: www.jobsintravelandtourism.co.uk

Journey Latin America (COMPANY)
Tel: 0161 832 1441
Website: www.journeylatinamerica.co.uk/home/jobs.shtml

Just4Aviation (WEBSITE)
Tel: 0845 050 2000
Website: www.just4aviation.net

Kumuka Worldwide (COMPANY)
Tel: 020 7937 8855
Website: www.kumuka.com

Kuoni (COMPANY)
Tel: 01306 744020
Website: www.kuoni.co.uk/Employment/index.html

Lastminute.com
Website: www.lastminute.com/lmn/aboutus/jobs.jhtml

Leisure Vacancies (WEBSITE)
Website: www.leisurevacancies.co.uk

Madventurer (COMPANY)
Tel: 0845 121 1996
Website: www.madventurer.com/jobs_at_mad.htm

Mark Warner Ltd (COMPANY)
Tel: 0870 033 0750
Website: www.markwarner-recruitment.co.uk

Mezzanine Recruitment (AGENCY)
Tel: 01903 237537
Website: www.mezzaninerecruitment.co.uk

MyTravel (COMPANY)
Website: www.mytravelcareers.co.uk

Natives (WEBSITE)
Tel: 020 8788 4271
Website: www.natives.co.uk/skijobs/default.htm

Neilson (COMPANY)
Tel: 0870 241 2901
Website: www.neilson.co.uk/Recruitment/index.asp

New Frontiers (AGENCY)
Tel: 0845 202 2222
Website: www.newfrontiers.co.uk

NST GROUP (COMPANY)
Tel: 01223 723456
Website: www.nstgroupjobs.co.uk

Olympic Holidays (COMPANY)
Tel: 0870 429 4141
Website: www.olympicholidays.com/information/recruitment.asp

Opodo (COMPANY)
Tel: 0870 352 5000
Website: www.opodo.com/careers/careers.html

Original Travel (COMPANY)
Tel: 020 7978 7333
Website: www.originaltravel.co.uk/about/employment

Overland Club (COMPANY)
Tel: 0845 658 0336
Website: www.overlandclub.com/employment.asp

Page & Moy (COMPANY)
Tel: 0870 833 4012
Website: www.page-moy.co.uk/careers.aspx

Peregrine Adventures (COMPANY)
Tel: 01635 872300
Website: www.peregrineadventures.com/about_us/employment.asp

PGL (COMPANY)
Tel: 0870 401 4411
Website: www.pgl.co.uk/online/workingwithpgl/index.asp

Prospects4Travel (AGENCY)
Tel: 020 7627 1919
Website: www.prospects4travel.com

Purple Ski (COMPANY)
Tel: 01885 488799
Website: www.purpleski.com/jobs/

Radical Travel Network (COMPANY)
Tel: 0131 557 9393
Website: www.shamrockertours.com

Ramblers Holidays (COMPANY)
Tel: 01707 331133
Website: www.ramblersholidays.co.uk

Real Gap (Company)
Tel: 01892 516164
Website: www.realgap.co.uk/Careers-at-Real-Gap

Resort Jobs (WEBSITE)
Tel: 0870 046 3377
Website: www.resortjobs.co.uk

Royal Caribbean Cruises International (COMPANY)
Tel: 01494 677125
Website: www.royalcaribbean.co.uk

Season Workers (WEBSITE)
Tel: 01383 723344
Website: www.seasonworkers.com/fe/

Secret Destinations (COMPANY)
Tel: 0845 612 9000
Website: www.secretdestinations.com

Skiworld (COMPANY)
Tel: 0870 420 5914/3
Website: www.skiworld.ltd.uk/index/form/Work_For_Us/
recruitment.php

SkyEurope Airlines (AIRLINE)
www2.skyeurope.com/EN/Default.aspx?CatID=81

STA Travel (COMPANY)
Tel: 0870 163 0026
Website: www.statravel.co.uk

Steppes Travel (COMPANY)
Tel: 01285 880980
Website: www.steppestravel.co.uk/job-opportunities-page126.aspx

Strong Recruitment (AGENCY)
Tel: 020 7493 2555
Website: www.strongrecruitment.co.uk

Sunvil Holidays (COMPANY)
Tel: 020 8568 4499
Website: www.sunvil.co.uk/sunvil/home/About_Sunvil/
Jobs_at_Sunvil.asp

T & T Travel Solutions Limited (WEBSITE)
Tel: 020 7382 1460
Website: www.t-ttrainingsolutions.co.uk/JobSearch.aspx

The Adventure Company (COMPANY)
Tel: 0870 794 1009
Website: www.adventurecompany.co.uk/work-for-us.aspx

The Camping and Caravanning Club (COMPANY)
Tel: 0845 130 7631
Website: www.campingandcaravanningclub.co.uk/jobs/

Thomas Cook (COMPANY)
Tel: 01733 416083
Website: www.thomascookjobs.co.uk

Thomson Holidays (COMPANY)
Tel: 0845 055 0255/8
Website: www.thomson.co.uk

Titan Travel (COMPANY)
Tel: 01293 455345
Website: www.titantravel.co.uk/jobs.asp

Top Language Jobs
Tel: 020 8363 3334
Website: www.toplanguagejobs.co.uk

Trailfinders (COMPANY)
Website: www.trailfinders.com/employment/recruitment.htm

TransIndus (COMPANY)
Tel: 020 8566 2729
Website: www.transindus.co.uk

Travel Industry Jobs (WEBSITE)
Tel: 0845 226 0770
Website: www.travelindustryjobs.co.uk

Travel Jobsearch.com (WEBSITE)
Tel: 01444 241177
Website: www.traveljobsearch.com

Travel Trade Recruitment (AGENCY)
Tel: 020 7953 1179
Website: www.traveltradejobs.com

Travel Weekly (WEBSITE)
Website: www.travelweekly.co.uk

Travel World Selection (AGENCY)
Tel: 0121 713 5990
Website: www.travelworldselection.co.uk

Travellers Worldwide (COMPANY)
Tel: 01903 502595
Website: www.travellersworldwide.com/job-vacancies.htm

Travelmood (COMPANY)
Tel: 0700 066 0004
Website: www.travelmood.com/site/about/careers/recruitment2006/careers.asp

Travelscope (COMPANY)
Tel: 0870 380 3333
Website: www.travelscope.co.uk/jobs.html

Travelsphere (COMPANY)
Tel: 0870 240 2428
Website: www.travelsphere.co.uk/website/about-trav/recruit-jobs.aspx

Viking Recruitment Limited (AGENCY)
Tel: 01304 240881
Website: www.vikingrecruitment.com

Virgin Holidays (COMPANY)
Website: www.virginholidays.co.uk/info/important/careers

Voovs.com (WEBSITE)
Tel: 020 7442 3456
Website: www.voovs.com

Wanderlust (WEBSITE)
Website: www.wanderlust.co.uk/jobshop/jobs01.html

Worldchoice (COMPANY)
Website: www.worldchoice.co.uk/employment.php

HELPFUL TRAINING ORGANISATIONS

TTENTO
People 1st
2nd Floor, Armstrong House
38 Market Square
Uxbridge
UB8 1LH
Tel: 0870 060 2550
Website: www.people1st.co.uk

Travel Training Company
The Quayside
4 Furnival Road
Sheffield
S4 7YA
Tel: 0800 915 9396
Website: www.ttctraining.co.uk

HELPFUL GENERAL CAREERS AND LEARNING INFORMATION

AGCAS (Association of Graduate Careers Advisory Services)
Millennium House
30 Junction Road
Sheffield
S11 8XB
Tel: 0114 251 5750
Website: www.agcas.org.uk

BASI (British Association of Snowsport Instructors)
Glenmore
Aviemore
PH22 1QU
Tel: 01479 861717
Website: www.basi.org.uk

CACHE (Council for Awards in Children's Care & Education)
Beaufort House
Grosvenor Road
St Albans
Hertfordshire
AL1 3AW
Tel: 01727 818616
Website: www.cache.org.uk

Career Development Loans
Tel: 0800 585 505
Website: www.direct.gov.uk/cdl

CILT (Centre for Information on Language Teaching & Research)
20 Bedfordbury
London
WC2N 4LB
Tel: 020 7379 5101
Website: www.cilt.org.uk

National Council for the Training of Journalists
The New Granary
Station Road
Newport
Saffron Walden
CB11 3PL
Tel: 01799 544014
www.nctj.com

Qualifications and Curriculum Authority
83 Piccadilly
London
W1J 8QA
Tel: 020 7509 5555
Website: www.qca.org.uk

Royal Geographical Society
1 Kensington Gore
London
SW7 2AR
Tel: 020 7591 3000
Website: www.rgs.org

UCAS (Universities and Colleges Admissions Service)
PO Box 28
Cheltenham
GL52 3LZ
Tel: 01242 222444
Website: www.ucas.com

HELPFUL PUBLICATIONS

MAGAZINES AND JOURNALS
Coach Monthly
Tel: 01926 455266
Website: www.cdc-coachmonthly.co.uk

Conference and Incentive Travel
Tel: 020 8627 4307
Website: www.citmagazine.com

Group Travel Organiser
Tel: 0845 166 8131
Website: www.grouptravelorganiser.com

Incentive Travel and Corporate Meetings
Tel: 0118 979 3277
Website: www.incentivetravel.co.uk

Travel Trade Gazette
Tel: 020 7921 8029
Website: www.ttglive.com

Travel Weekly
Tel: 01444 475606
Website: www.travelweekly.co.uk

TravelMole (online news)
Website: www.travelmole.com

HELPFUL

TRAVEL CAREERS

Careers and jobs in travel and tourism, Verite Reily Collins (Kogan Page, 2004)
ISBN: 0 7494 4205 0

Becoming a Tour Guide, Verite Reily Collins (Thomson Learning, 2000)
ISBN: 0 8264 4788 0

GNVQ Intermediate Leisure and Tourism, Stephen Pearson, Sandra Nichol, Katherine Kemp (Longman, 2000)
ISBN: 0 582 38162 2

Real Life Guide to Passenger Transport, Bob Lees (Trotman, 2006)
ISBN: 1 84455 109 1

Working on Cruise Ships, Sandra Bow (Vacation Work Publications, 2005)
ISBN: 1 854 58338 7

GENERAL CAREERS BOOKS

Careers 2007 (Trotman, 2006)
ISBN: 1 84455 080 X

Winning CVs for First-time Job Hunters, Kathleen Houston (Trotman, 2004)
ISBN: 0 85660 971 4

Winning Interviews for First-time Job Hunters, Kathleen Houston (Trotman, 2004)
ISBN: 0 85660 972 2